Cu   Ca

This Book Belongs to

_____

Cursive Cats

ACTIVITY BOOK FOR KIDS

70 Activities Including Coloring, Dot-to-Dots & Spot the Difference

Valerie Deneen

ILLUSTRATED BY
Laura Watkins

ROCKRIDGE
PRESS

Interior and Cover Designer: Karmen Lizzul
Art Producer: Sue Bischofberger
Editors: Elizabeth Baird and Eliza Kirby
Production Editor: Andrew Yackira
Illustration © 2020 Laura Watkins

ISBN: Print 978-1-64739-611-4
R0

Draw a picture of your cat
(or a cat you want).

WELCOME!

If you love cats and enjoy activities, this is the book for you! This book is filled with pictures to color and fun activities to do. You will learn lots of interesting facts about cats and cat care while doing word search puzzles, mazes, dot-to-dots, and more!

ALL ABOUT
MY FAVORITE CAT AND ME

My name is _____.

I am _____ years old.

I love cats because _____.

If I had a cat, I would name it _____.

My favorite type of cat is a _____

because _____.

Some activities I do with my cat are _____,

_____, and _____.

If my cat could talk, I would ask it _____.

My favorite place to take my cat would be _____

because _____.

My favorite book to read to my cat would be _____

by _____.

My cat's favorite treat would be _____.

Shopping for Supplies

With proper care, cats can be great friends! The words in this list are items from the pet supply store. Can you find all 5 words hidden in the puzzle? Words are hidden three ways: from left to right, up to down, and diagonal from left to right.

FOOD   TREATS   TOYS

BED   DISH

L W W N N A A N X T
E R V G D I S H B R
S L D T F K A U L E
Y M B L E L P Q T A
V T Y R A H J B F T
H C O L E B E D O S
J F B Y L F Q R H V
R M X D S W O U R I
U W S I D W E O N R
Y D H A F U D F D Y

See page 76 for the answer key!

This tabby cat loves to play with its ball toy!

Think Outside the Box

Many cats enjoy playing in empty cardboard boxes! Help guide this tuxedo cat through the maze of boxes to find its food bowl.

See page 76 for the answer key!

Fun with Feathers

This calico kitten wants to play! Connect the dots to make a fun feather toy.

See page 76 for the answer key!

Purrfect Posts

Scratching posts give your cat a place to sharpen its claws without damaging the furniture! Can you spot the 5 differences between these two pictures?

See page 76 for the answer key!

These orange tabby cats live in a bookstore and greet customers at the door!

Adoption Day

This Russian blue kitten has just been adopted and is excited to explore its new home! What's strange about this picture? Circle all 4 things that are wrong.

See page 76 for the answer key!

So Many Cat-egories

There are many different types of cats! Can you find all 5 hidden in the puzzle? Words are hidden three ways: from left to right, up to down, and diagonal from left to right.

SHORTHAIR   SPHYNX   SIAMESE

RAGDOLL   PERSIAN

G S E H B W R H H N
S P P E R S I A N R
R H V J C U W V S P
A Y O W O I H K I C
G N F R O L P J A M
D X Q T T N T O M Y
O I N W R H Y P E P
L J Z R F F A B S E
L U U B T A K I E G
P L U M A P V T R G

See page 76 for the answer key!

Playful Persians

For healthy exercise, these Persian kittens love to run and chase each other in the garden! Can you find all 5 things hidden in the picture below?

 Teapot   Lollipop   Paintbrush

Ruler   Heart

See page 76 for the answer key!

Cats need fresh food and water every day. This short-haired cat looks forward to mealtime!

Finish

Treats

Start

Pawsome Exercise!

Cats love to run through tunnels! Help this Ragdoll cat through the tunnel maze to find some tasty treats.

See page 76 for the answer key!

Pretty Pawtraits

Can you finish the portrait of this Himalayan cat to add to the museum display?

Spot the Difference

Bengal cats have spots called "rosettes" that are also found on wildcats such as leopards or jaguars! Can you find all 5 differences between the patterns on these two Bengal cats?

See page 76 for the answer key!

Polydactyl cats are also known as "thumb cats" because they have extra toes!

Cute Collar

This Snowshoe cat is excited to get its new collar! Connect the dots to help place the collar around its neck.

See page 77 for the answer key!

Cap-purr-ccino

These cats live in a cat café and have regular visitors who love to play and cuddle with them. Can you find all 6 things hidden in this cat café?

Bat

Feather

Comb

Banana

Pizza

Cake

See page 77 for the answer key!

Cat-tivities

Cats can do many activities! Can you find all 6 words hidden in the puzzle? Words are hidden three ways: from left to right, up to down, and diagonal from left to right.

NAP   MEOW   JUMP

EAT   PURR   PLAY

K Q D I J U M P F O

L Y A S T P E L Z I

M C I V X U M A B E

E S H L A R E Y V Z

A Y U J L R O V K X

G L V H P D W O R U

K M A S G Z G F L P

D F E E Y J L N X A

B W A L Q L Z I A G

E N T U J O I E D P

See page 77 for the answer key!

Bengal cats are very active and need a safe space to jump and play.

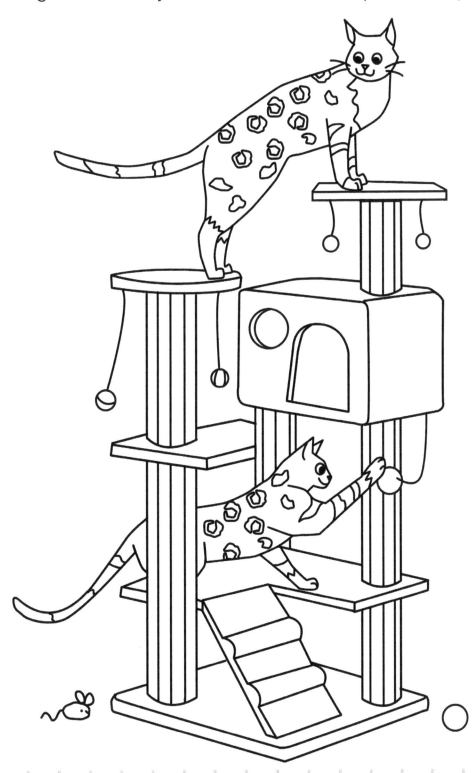

Finish

Start

Kitten Cuteness

This kitten is looking for its litter of brothers and sisters! Help guide it through the garden maze to find the basket with its sleeping siblings.

See page 77 for the answer key!

Feline Fine

These cats are napping by the fireplace. What's strange about this picture? Circle all 3 things that are out of place.

See page 77 for the answer key!

Toy Time!

These two cats have lots of toys. Can you spot all 6 differences between the two pictures?

See page 77 for the answer key!

An empty paper bag is one of this Maine coon cat's favorite toys!

Acro-cat-ics

This cat is competing in an agility show! Can you guide it through the maze of obstacles to the first-place prize ribbon?

See page 77 for the answer key!

Whimsical Whiskers

Cats have sensitive whiskers that can pick up small changes in airflow. Connect the dots to complete the cat around its whiskers!

See page 77 for the answer key!

Parts of a Cat

These words are parts of a cat's body. Can you find all 6 words hidden in the puzzle? Words are hidden three ways: from left to right, up to down, and diagonal from left to right.

PAWS   WHISKER   TAIL

CLAW   FUR   MUZZLE

S K M U Z Z L E O S
X T Q P Y M P A W S
T M R V G D J B Q H
Q V V K X Z Y T A E
W H I S K E R Q P Z
C I Z P K Y A E F Y
G L T Q E P F A N L
L H A X A N U U K C
L S I W V H R Y H K
L Y L N L A V C X Y

See page 77 for the answer key!

Japanese bobtail cats are born with short rabbitlike tails. They are said to bring good luck to those who live with them.

Cats Are Ah-mazing!

This Bombay cat is looking for its catnip toy! Can you guide it through the cardboard box maze so it can play?

See page 78 for the answer key!

Singapura cats are one of the smallest cat breeds.
They are known for their large ears and eyes.

Kitten Palooza

It's a kitten adoption event! Can you find all 6 items hidden in the picture below?

Cat food bowl	Tennis ball	Carrot
Party hat	Cake	Pen

See page 78 for the answer key!

Purrfect Playroom

Abyssinian cats have lots of energy and love to play! Can you draw some cat toys for this Abyssinian cat?

Sleepy Siamese Kittens

These Siamese kittens have been playing all day and want to take a nap. Connect the dots to make a cozy bed for them!

Sphynx cats do not have any hair. This sphynx cat likes to wear fluffy sweaters!

Life's a Stage

Cats go through several stages as they grow. Can you find all 6 words hidden in the puzzle? Words are hidden three ways: from left to right, up to down, and diagonal from left to right.

KITTEN   JUNIOR   PRIME

SENIOR   MATURE   GERIATRIC

W M K I T T E N G L
J S C Q S B M Y E P
L U F D D G A Z R R
S E N I V F T C I I
C G S I Q M U Z A M
D W U E O Y R V T E
Z E O W N R E O R G
X K D N K I L L I A
V R A O H A O Y C X
I J D I B I L R U N

See page 78 for the answer key!

Cardboard Kingdom

Cats love to play, sleep, and hide in cardboard boxes! Draw an epic cardboard castle for this Turkish Angora cat to enjoy.

Finish

Start

Walk Me Right Meow!

This mixed breed cat can't wait to go for a walk in a stroller! Help guide the stroller through the park maze.

See page 78 for the answer key!

Hungry Felines

These foster kittens are hungry after playing all day.
Connect the dots to make a food dish so they can eat!

Garden Cat-astrophe!

These cats are playing in the garden! What's wrong with this picture? Circle all 6 things that are out of place.

See page 78 for the answer key!

44

These tabby kittens get plenty of exercise playing with their activity center!

Clever Cat Trees

Cats need space to jump and play. Connect the dots to draw a cat tree for this cat to enjoy!

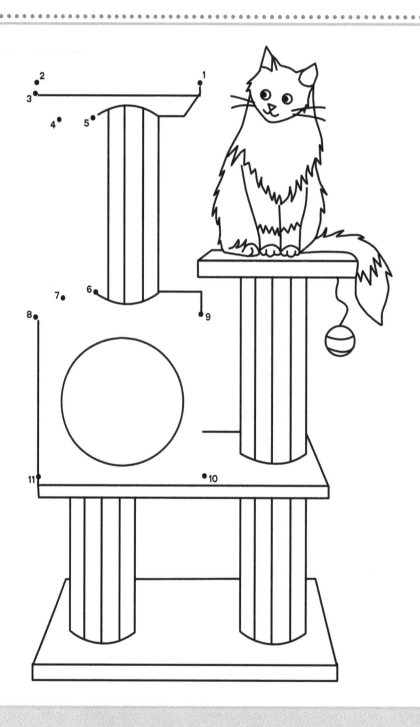

This Burmese cat plays with its rope toy!

Caring for Cats

Adoption centers work hard to find forever homes for cats. Can you find the 7 words hidden in the puzzle? Words are hidden three ways: from left to right, up to down, and diagonal from left to right.

ADOPT	SHELTER	FOSTER
CLINIC	VET	CARE
	FEED	

```
X Z A D O P T V O P
P X C I G P G R F O
W C B L S M V M X E
T I A F I J Y J F W
E F Q R O N T H E B
V F U U E S I W E Q
Q E D P H Q T C D U
B K T M K D A E R V
A S H E L T E R R A
B Q B A E Y M H J C
```

See page 78 for the answer key!

This barn cat lives in a stable and enjoys the company of horses!

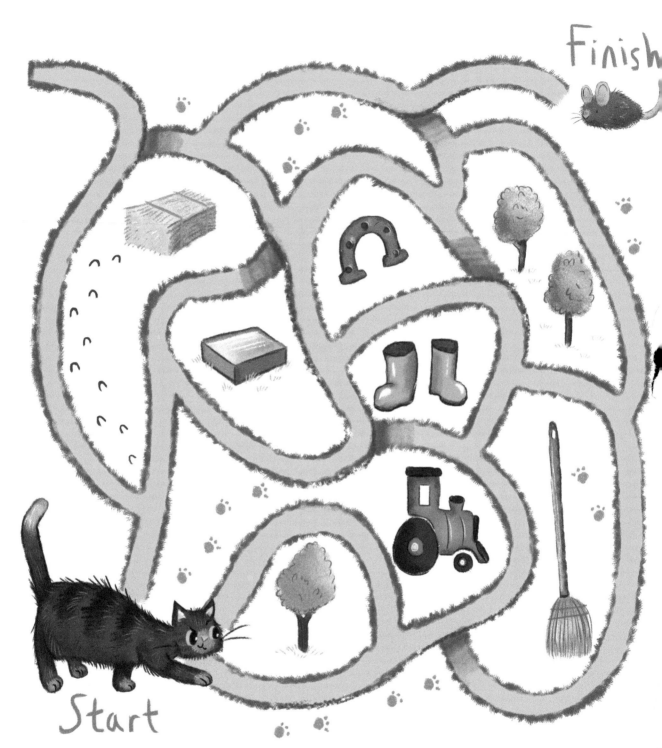

Finish

Start

Helpful Hunters

Barn cats are helpful hunters on a farm. Help this barn cat through the farm maze to catch the mouse.

See page 79 for the answer key!

Here's Looking at You, Cat

This Scottish fold cat is looking in the mirror. Can you draw what it sees?

Special Spots

Every calico cat has its own special fur pattern. Can you find all 7 differences between these two pictures?

See page 79 for the answer key!

This cat has been trained to give high fives!

In-tents Napping

This cat wants a hiding place for a nap. Connect the dots to make a cozy tent for it!

See page 79 for the answer key!

Furever Homes

This animal shelter is hosting an adoption event for cats to find their forever homes! Can you find all 7 items hidden in the picture?

 Envelope   Domino   Watch   Heart

 Bell   Hat   Carrot

See page 79 for the answer key!

Furends Furever

Cats can have many different fur patterns! Often their name gives a hint about their fur pattern. Can you find all 7 words hidden in the puzzle? Words are hidden three ways: from left to right, up to down, and diagonal from left to right.

TABBY   TORTIE   SOLID

SPOTTED   TUXEDO   STRIPED

       CALICO

```
H  L  F  T  O  R  T  I  E  H
C  T  S  U  W  B  S  P  Y  S
F  A  O  D  S  F  L  N  C  P
N  Y  L  S  T  R  I  P  E  D
T  O  I  I  P  U  R  J  X  L
R  A  D  P  C  O  X  G  E  I
D  W  B  G  U  O  T  E  J  Q
T  Q  L  B  T  U  L  T  D  I
D  J  P  Z  Y  D  J  Y  E  O
P  U  K  A  T  M  J  N  Q  D
```

See page 79 for the answer key!

These two cats enjoy playing patty-cake together!

Sleep in a Sunbeam

A sunbeam makes a cozy napping spot for a cat. Can you help guide this domestic cat through the maze to find the sunny window?

See page 79 for the answer key!

These foster kittens love to cuddle together for naps.

A Silly Shop

This black cat lives in a bike shop. What's wrong with this picture? Circle all 4 things that are out of place.

See page 79 for the answer key!

Slow eye-blinking is a cat's way of blowing kisses!

Tell Tail Sign

If a cat greets you with its tail straight up, it is a sign of respect. Connect the dots to give this cat its tail.

Tasty Treats

Draw your cat's favorite treat!

Tricky Tunnel

A tunnel can be a great toy for a cat. Can you help guide this ginger cat through the tunnel maze to find the cat treats?

See page 79 for the answer key!

Purrfect Patterns

Cats can have lots of different colors and patterns! Can you find all 8 differences between these cats?

See page 80 for the answer key!

Wild about Big Cats

The cats in this list are big cats that live in the wild. Can you find all 7 words hidden in the puzzle? Words are hidden three ways: from left to right, up to down, and diagonal from left to right.

LION	LYNX	COUGAR
JAGUAR	LEOPARD	
TIGER	CHEETAH	

R O Y C Y N W C A L
Q W V O L V U W N Y
Y F C U E I Z X D N
M I T G O C L W W X
B U I A P H Q I S D
Z Q G R A E Q P O R
M J E R R E P A P N
V F R C D T U S L G
U J A G U A R Q J D
P J L E U H N J I B

See page 80 for the answer key!

66

This Russian blue cat is stretching after enjoying an afternoon nap.

That's How Eye Roll

Cats' eyes have pupils that help them see well even in very low light! Connect the dots to complete the drawing of the cat's eye.

Showtime!

This Bengal cat is competing in an agility show! Can you find all 7 things hidden in the picture?

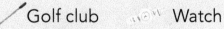 Music note   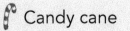 Candy cane   Golf club   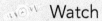 Watch

 Pizza   Pencil   Snake

See page 80 for the answer key!

Feline Fine

Cats are one of the most popular pets in the world! Can you find all 8 words hidden in the puzzle? Words are hidden three ways: from left to right, up to down, and diagonal from left to right.

CARE	EXERCISE	TREAT
CATNIP	MEOW	LITTER
KITTEN	PURR	

```
J  K  U  L  R  Q  P  Z  E  P
K  C  A  T  N  I  P  A  F  W
I  L  R  Q  I  T  R  E  A  T
T  I  W  W  R  I  E  X  Q  Z
T  T  B  M  I  C  A  E  A  P
E  T  M  W  Y  A  P  R  W  A
N  E  U  E  N  R  U  C  R  R
H  R  N  G  O  E  R  I  J  R
J  J  N  B  A  W  R  S  A  K
B  R  Y  S  F  P  G  E  G  B
```

See page 80 for the answer key!

This short-haired cat has been trained to ride a skateboard!

Finish

start

Walk to Water

Cats need plenty of clean, fresh water available at all times. Help this thirsty calico cat through the maze to the water bowl.

See page 80 for the answer key!

Fun with Fosters

Foster kittens can be very active! What's wrong with this picture? Circle all 8 things that are out of place.

See page 80 for the answer key!

Brushed and Beautiful

Long-haired cats need to be brushed regularly. Can you connect the dots to draw a brush for this long-haired cat?

See page 80 for the answer key!

Kittens born to the same litter can have different colors and markings.

Answer Key

Shopping for Supplies
With proper care, cats can be great friends! The words in this list are items from the pet supply store. Can you find all 5 words hidden in the puzzle? Words are hidden three ways: from left to right, up to down, and diagonal from left to right.

FOOD   TREATS   TOYS
BED   DISH

Think Outside the Box
Many cats enjoy playing in empty cardboard boxes! Help guide this tuxedo cat through the maze of boxes to find its food bowl.

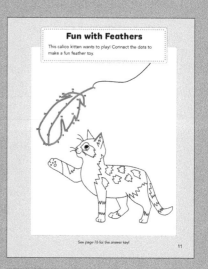

Fun with Feathers
This calico kitten wants to play! Connect the dots to make a fun feather toy.

Purrfect Posts
Scratching posts give your cat a place to sharpen its claws without damaging the furniture! Can you spot the 5 differences between these two pictures?

Adoption Day
This Russian blue kitten has just been adopted and is excited to explore its new home! What's strange about this picture? Circle all 4 things that are wrong.

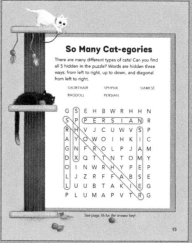

So Many Cat-egories
There are many different types of cats! Can you find all 5 hidden in the puzzle? Words are hidden three ways: from left to right, up to down, and diagonal from left to right.

SHORTHAIR   SPHYNX   SIAMESE
RAGDOLL   PERSIAN

Playful Persians
For healthy exercise, these Persian kittens love to run and chase each other in the garden! Can you find all 5 things hidden in the picture below?

Teapot   Lollipop   Paintbrush
Ruler   Heart

Pawsome Exercise!
Cats love to run through tunnels! Help this Ragdoll cat through the tunnel maze to find some tasty treats.

Spot the Difference
Bengal cats have spots called "rosettes" that are also found on wildcats such as leopards or jaguars! Can you find all 5 differences between the patterns on these two Bengal cats?

Answer Key

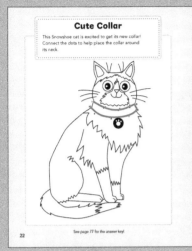

Cute Collar
This Snowshoe cat is excited to get its new collar! Connect the dots to help place the collar around its neck.

22   See page 77 for the answer key!

Cap-purr-ccino
These cats live in a cat café and have regular visitors who love to play and cuddle with them. Can you find all 6 things hidden in this cat café?

- Bat
- Banana
- Feather
- Pizza
- Comb
- Cake

See page 77 for the answer key!   23

Cat-tivities
Cats can do many activities! Can you find all 6 words hidden in the puzzle? Words are hidden three ways: from left to right, up to down, and diagonal from left to right.

NAP   MEOW   JUMP
EAT   PURR   PLAY

24   See page 77 for the answer key!

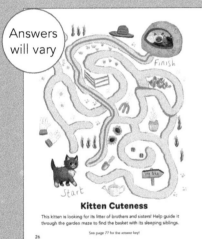

Answers will vary

Start

Finish

Kitten Cuteness
This kitten is looking for its litter of brothers and sisters! Help guide it through the garden maze to find the basket with its sleeping siblings.

26   See page 77 for the answer key!

Feline Fine
These cats are napping by the fireplace. What's strange about this picture? Circle all 3 things that are out of place.

See page 77 for the answer key!   27

Toy Time!
These two cats have lots of toys. Can you spot all 6 differences between the two pictures?

28   See page 77 for the answer key!

Finish

Start

Acro-cat-ics
This cat is competing in an agility show! Can you guide maze of obstacles to the first-place prize ribbon?

Answers will vary

30   See page 77 for the answer key!

Whimsical Whiskers
Cats have sensitive whiskers that can pick up small changes in airflow. Connect the dots to complete the cat around its whiskers!

See page 77 for the answer key!   31

Parts of a Cat
These words are parts of a cat's body. Can you find all 6 words hidden in the puzzle? Words are hidden three ways: from left to right, up to down, and diagonal from left to right.

PAWS   WHISKER   TAIL
CLAW   FUR   MUZZLE

32   See page 78 for the answer key!

Answer Key

Answers will vary

Cats Are Ah-mazing!
This Bombay cat is looking for its catnip toy! Can you guide it through the cardboard box maze so it can play?

See page 78 for the answer key!

34

Kitten Palooza
It's a kitten adoption event! Can you find all 6 items hidden in the picture below?

- Cat food bowl
- Tennis ball
- Carrot
- Party hat
- Cake
- Pen

See page 78 for the answer key!

36

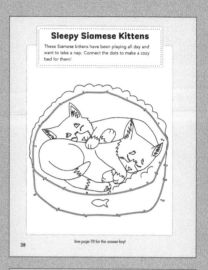

Sleepy Siamese Kittens
These Siamese kittens have been playing all day and want to take a nap. Connect the dots to make a cozy bed for them!

See page 78 for the answer key!

38

Life's a Stage
Cats go through several stages as they grow. Can you find all 6 words hidden in the puzzle? Words are hidden three ways: from left to right, up to down, and diagonal from left to right.

KITTEN   JUNIOR   PRIME

SENIOR   MATURE   GERIATRIC

See page 78 for the answer key!

40

Walk Me Right M...
This mixed breed cat can't wait to go for a walk i... the stroller through the park maze.

Answers will vary

See page 78 for the answer key!

42

Hungry Felines
These foster kittens are hungry after playing all day. Connect the dots to make a food dish so they can eat!

See page 78 for the answer key!

43

Garden Cat-astrophe!
These cats are playing in the garden! What's wrong with this picture? Circle all 6 things that are out of place.

See page 78 for the answer key!

44

Clever Cat Trees
Cats need space to jump and play. Connect the dots to draw a cat tree for this cat to enjoy!

See page 78 for the answer key!

46

Caring for Cats
Adoption centers work hard to find forever homes for cats. Can you find the 7 words hidden in the puzzle? Words are hidden three ways: from left to right, up to down, and diagonal from left to right.

ADOPT   SHELTER   FOSTER

CLINIC   VET   CARE

FEED

See page 78 for the answer key!

48

Answer Key

Answers will vary

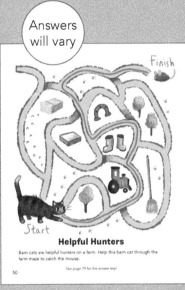

Helpful Hunters

Barn cats are helpful hunters on a farm. Help this barn cat through the farm maze to catch the mouse.

50   See page 79 for the answer key!

Special Spots

Every calico cat has its own special fur pattern. Can you find all 7 differences between these two pictures?

52   See page 79 for the answer key!

In-tents Napping

This cat wants a hiding place for a nap. Connect the dots to make a cozy tent for it!

54   See page 79 for the answer key!

Furever Homes

This animal shelter is hosting an adoption event for cats to find their forever homes! Can you find all 7 items hidden in the picture?

Envelope   Domino   Watch   Heart
Bell   Hat   Carrot

See page 79 for the answer key!   55

Furends Furever

Cats can have many different fur patterns! Often their name gives a hint about their fur pattern. Can you find all 7 words hidden in the puzzle? Words are hidden three ways: from left to right, up to down, and diagonal from left to right.

TABBY   TORTIE   SOLID
SPOTTED   TUXEDO   STRIPED
CALICO

See page 79 for the answer key!

56

Sleep in a Sunbeam

A sunbeam makes a cozy napping spot for a cat. Can you help guide this domestic cat through the maze to find the sunny window?

58   See page 79 for the answer key!

A Silly Shop

This black cat lives in a bike shop. What's wrong with this picture? Circle all 4 things that are out of place.

60   See page 79 for the answer key!

Tell Tail Sign

If a cat greets you with its tail straight up, it is a sign of respect. Connect the dots to give this cat its tail.

62   See page 79 for the answer key!

Tricky Tunnel

A tunnel can be a great toy for a cat. Can you help guide this ginger cat through the tunnel maze to find the cat treats?

64   See page 80 for the answer key!

Answer Key

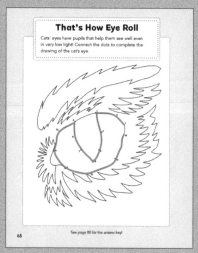

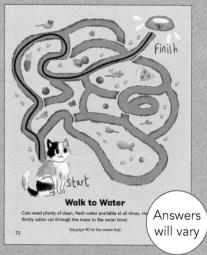

Answers will vary

ABOUT THE AUTHOR

VALERIE DENEEN is the founder of InnerChildFun.com, where she writes about what to do with kids, creative play for all ages, parenting tips and tricks, learning and educational activities for kids, craft ideas for tweens and school-aged children, and gardening with kids. Valerie is a speaker, creative play advocate, brand ambassador, television personality, and active Rotarian. Her work has been featured in *High Five* magazine, *FamilyFun* magazine, PBS Parents, various morning talk shows, and several online publications. For creative play ideas sent directly to your inbox, visit Valerie's blog at InnerChildFun.com and subscribe to the weekly newsletter.

ABOUT THE ILLUSTRATOR

LAURA WATKINS is an illustrator living in London. Her studio is based in Finchley and houses a collection of towering books, paints, and pencils. Since graduating from UCA in 2011, Laura has been lucky enough to work on a variety of exciting projects. She has spent time working in galleries, created lines of greetings cards, and illustrated enough books to fill a shelf. One of her latest published books, *T is For Tiger*, became an Amazon best seller. Laura primarily works digitally but does enjoy getting all the paints out and has painted animals onto the walls of the NHS children's hospital in Lambeth. Laura now runs a boutique dog print shop, Watkins Prints, which is the perfect match for an animal lover.